Delaney
Street
Press

A Child's Book
of Wisdom

A Child's Book
of Wisdom

by Dr. Criswell Freeman

DELANEY STREET PRESS
Nashville, TN
1-800-256-8584

ISBN: 1-58334-060-2

The quoted ideas expressed in this book are not, in all cases, exact quotations, as some have been edited for clarity and brevity. In all cases, the author has attempted to maintain the speaker's original intent. In some cases, quoted material for this book was obtained from secondary sources, primarily print media. While every effort was made to ensure the accuracy of these sources, the accuracy cannot be guaranteed. For additions, deletions, corrections or clarifications in future editions of this text, please write DELANEY STREET PRESS.

Printed in the United States of America.

Layout by Criswell Freeman
1 2 3 4 5 6 7 8 9 10 • 00 01 02 03 03 04 05

Acknowledgments

The author acknowledges the helpful support of Angela Beasley Freeman, Dick and Mary Freeman, Mary Susan Freeman, Jim Gallery and Margaret Queen.

For Marie Carlisle Freeman

Table of Contents

 11

A Note About
The Quotes

This book is a collection of ideas from some of history's wisest men and women. But, it is also a book for young people, so I have taken the liberty of changing the wording of several quotations in this book. By doing so, I have attempted to make these timeless principles more easily understood by kids of all ages.

This book is intended to be read and discussed by parents and children. Hopefully, the ideas on these pages will spark a love of great thoughts and great quotations. If so, this book has served its purpose.

The Author

Chapter 1

Being Kind to Other People

It's important to be kind to other people. When you are kind, you know you've done the right thing, and that makes you feel better about yourself. So always remember the Golden Rule: Treat others like you want to be treated.

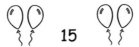

Always be a little kinder than necessary.

Sir James Barrie

Sir James Barrie was a writer
from Scotland. He understood that
kindness costs nothing
but is priceless.

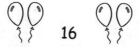

Be kind to everybody you meet... you never know what kind of troubles others might have.

Philo

Philo lived a long time ago in Rome. His words are still true because kindness never goes out of style.

A person wrapped up in himself.......

.... makes ....

a very small
package.

Ben Franklin

Franklin was an American writer
statesman, publisher, and inventor.

No act of kindness, no matter how small, is ever wasted.

Aesop

Aesop was a legendary Greek storyteller who probably lived about 2500 years ago. He created the stories we know as Aesop's Fables.

When you do good things for other people, it makes you feel good inside!

Maurice Maeterlinck

Mister Maeterlinck was a Belgian writer who won a contest called the Nobel Prize. He understood that good deeds lead to good feelings.

Kind words can be short and easy to speak, but their echoes are truly endless.

Mother Teresa

Mother Teresa was a Christian missionary who opened schools for poor children in Calcutta, India. Her kind words continue to echo.

22

Chapter 2

Doing What's Right

Sometimes, you face a choice: "Should I do the right thing, or not?" Maybe it's easier to do something you know is wrong. But bad behavior always leads to BIG TROUBLE. So the next time you have a choice, do the right thing ... you won't be sorry.

Every day you
are becoming
what you are
going to be.

Samuel Johnson

Also known as "Dr. Johnson," Samuel
was a famous English writer who
lived in the 1700's.

Do the best you can with what you have where you are.

Teddy Roosevelt

Teddy Roosevelt was the 26th president of the United States. The Teddy Bear is named in his honor.

Do you want to be happy? Do what you know is right!

George Washington

George Washington was the
very first president of the
United States. He understood
that happiness and goodness
go hand-in-hand.

Your behavior is a picture of yourself.

Goethe

Goethe was a German writer and poet who who was born in 1749. Even back then, good behavior was smart behavior.

With every deed, you are sowing a seed.

Ella Wheeler Wilcox

Ella Wheeler Wilcox was a popular American poet who gained fame in the late 19th century.

The reward of a good deed is to have done it.

Seneca

Seneca was a philosopher who lived about two thousand years ago. A philosopher is someone who teaches us about life.

Be sure you're right, then go ahead!
Davy Crockett

Davy Crockett was an American pioneer who lived in Tennessee and fought at the Battle of the Alamo in Texas.

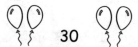

Chapter 3
Telling the Truth

When you tell the truth, people quickly learn to trust what you say. But if you make a habit of not telling the truth, you become like the boy who cried "wolf." So be truthful, even when it's hard. You'll soon learn that honesty is always the best policy. Honest!

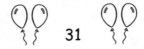

When in doubt...

.....tell the truth!

Mark Twain

Mark Twain was an American writer. He wrote *The Adventures of Tom Sawyer*.

Honesty is the first chapter in the book of wisdom.

Thomas Jefferson

Jefferson was the third president of the United States, and he wrote the Declaration of Independence.

The best time
to tell the truth...

is always now.

Albert Schweitzer

Schweitzer was a French missionary,
philosopher, and doctor. For much
of his life, he worked in Africa.

Honesty makes up for so many mistakes.

Sojourner Truth

Sojourner Truth was an American reformer. Reformers work to change things for the better.

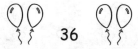

When you tell the truth, you don't have to remember what it was that you said.

Jewish Proverb

A proverb is a saying that reminds us of something important... like telling the truth.

The truth will make you free.

The Bible
John 8:32

Every time you tell the truth,
it's like lighting a candle
in the darkness.

38

Chapter 4

When You Make a Mistake

Everybody makes mistakes and you will too. Don't worry about trying to be perfect. When you make a mistake, fix it and learn from it. Anybody can make a mistake once, but it takes a very wise person to make it once and only once.

39

Our mistakes are our teachers.

Horace

Horace was a poet who lived about 2,000 years ago. He understood that mistakes can teach us important lessons.

40

Hardships are wonderful because they make us strong.

Lawrence Welk

Mr. Welk was an American bandleader and TV star. He realized that hard times can make us stronger.

Failure isn't falling down...

A Child's Book of Wisdom

..it's staying down.

Mary Pickford

Mary Pickford was a movie star during the early days of Hollywood. And, judging by her words, she was also a wise and determined woman.

The very biggest mistake you can make is to always be fearing you will make one.

Elbert Hubbard

Hubbard was an American writer and publisher.

44

If you do many things, you will make many mistakes, but you will not make the biggest mistake of all: doing nothing.

Ben Franklin

Franklin published *Poor Richard's Almanac* for many years.

Never let the fear of striking out get in your way.
Babe Ruth

Babe Ruth was one of the greatest home run hitters in the history of baseball.

Chapter 5

Having Fun

Every kid deserves to have lots of fun and that includes <u>you</u>! So make today, and every day "Fun day." It's the best day of the week.

Most people are about as happy as they make up their minds to be.

Abraham Lincoln

"Honest Abe" Lincoln was an American president who knew that happiness is simply another form of wisdom.

48

Play happy!
Willie Mays

Willie Mays was a great baseball
player. He understood that the
reason to play a game is
to have fun!

Life is what you make it....

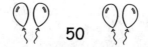

...always has been, always will be.

Grandma Moses

Grandma Moses was a famous artist. She didn't start her painting career until she was 75 years old!

51

Laughter comes from God.

Sophocles

Sophocles lived in Greece 2500
years ago. He wrote plays
for a living.

Laughter is God's medicine.

Henry Ward Beecher

Mister Beecher was a preacher,
and he knew that laughter
can be a wise teacher.

What sunshine is to flowers, smiles are to people.

Joseph Addison

Mr. Addison was a British writer who understood the importance of a smiling face and a kind word.

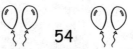

54

Laugh and the world laughs with you.

Ella Wheeler Wilcox

Ella Wheeler Wilcox was correct: When we laugh out loud, our friends are quick to join in.

Happiness is a duty that is underrated. Everybody owes it to themselves to be happy.

Robert Louis Stevenson

Mister Stevenson was a Scottish writer who understood that you deserve to be happy. Now!

56

A Child's Book of Wisdom

God's in his heaven. All's right with the world!

Robert Browning

Browning was born in London, England in the year 1812. He was a poet.

Chapter 6
Taking Care of Yourself

You've heard it from grown-ups lots of times: "Be careful!" Why are grown people so concerned about your safety? Because they love you, and they know kids can and do get hurt. So be careful...PLEASE!

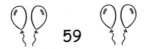

Better safe than sorry!

Old-time Saying

If you're not sure if it's safe to
do something, don't do it.

Look before you leap!

Old-time Saying

Even when you're playing, keep your eyes open and think about safety.

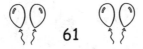

Know how to say "no."

Baltasar Gracián

Gracián was a priest who understood
that when people want us to do
dangerous things,
we must say "no!"

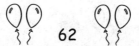

In the end, trust your feelings.

Ralph Waldo Emerson

Emerson was an American
writer who knew that our
feelings can give us wise advice
about right and wrong.

 63

Your heart
sees before
your eyes do.

Thomas Carlyle

If you have a feeling that
something is dangerous,
trust that feeling.

Chapter 7
Minding Your Manners

People will get to
know you by the way
you behave. And if
you want to be known
as a nice person,
you'll learn to mind
your manners.
Here's how...

Bad manners spoil everything.

Baltasar Gracián

When you misbehave, it makes
trouble for everybody,
especially you..................

66

Good manners are the fruit of a wise mind.

Alfred, Lord Tennyson

............That's why wise people mind their manners.

Treat all the people you meet with respect.

Confucius

Confucius was a Chinese philosopher who lived 2500 years ago. Even back then, good manners were important.

Never make fun of other people.

Mack Sennett

In the early days of Hollywood, Mr. Sennett made movies. His movies were funny, but this advice is serious.

Sow seeds of kindness.

George Ade

When you plant the seed of kindness, you reap a friend.

A Child's Book of Wisdom

Goodness
never fails.

Henry David Thoreau

When in doubt, be nice.

71

Your behavior is a picture of yourself.

Goethe

So why not make that picture a beautiful one?

Chapter 7
Making Friends

Our friends can help make us happy. But how do we make and keep good friends? Well, we can start by taking the advice on the pages that follow.

A friend is a present you give to yourself.

Robert Louis Stevenson

We can make our world happy
by choosing the right friends.

74

A good way to
make a new
friend is
to become
interested in
that person.

Dale Carnegie

Mr. Carnegie wrote a book
called "How to Win Friends and
Influence People."

 75

A cheerful friend is like a sunny day.

John Lubbock

A smiling friend, like a beautiful day, can make you happy.

Laughter improves everything.

James Thurber

Laughter makes everything
better, especially friendships.

We make friends by praising them.

Oliver Wendell Holmes, Sr.

Holmes was an American doctor who understood that praise is a powerful medicine.

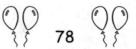

Treat your friends like you want your friends to treat you.

Aristotle

Aristotle lived in Greece about 2500 years ago. His advice is as important today as it was then.

Love others as much as you love yourself.

The Bible
Galatians 5:14

This is truly the golden rule of friendship.

Chapter 8
Your Family

Nothing is more important to you than your family. A loving family is a wonderful blessing and a reason to be thankful. Remember to tell your family members that you love them.

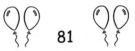

A happy family is like heaven on earth.

Sir John Bowring

You can do your part to make
the family happy.

Whenever the family is together, we feel at peace.

Russian Proverb

When you're with your family and all is well, be thankful!

83

In times of test, family is best.

Old Saying

We depend upon our family members, and they depend upon us.

The happiest times are the times we spend with family.

Thomas Jefferson

Family time is important for many reasons, not the least of which is because it's fun.

85

Ask yourself if you're behaving in a way that you would want your child to behave if you were the parent.

Charles Kingsley

You family deserves
your best behavior.

Chapter 10
Thinking Good Thoughts

How you think determines how you feel. Here's some good advice for thinking better and feeling better.

A happy heart is like a medicine.

The Bible
Proverbs 17:22

A happy heart helps keep you
healthy.

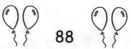

The best part of health is a happy mind.

Ralph Waldo Emerson

An important part of healthy living is healthy thinking.

A happy heart is a lasting blessing.

Ovid

Ovid was a Latin poet who understood the importance of happiness.

Learn how to be happy.

Seneca

Seneca, like Ovid, lived about 2000 years ago. Seneca understood that we can teach ourselves to be happy people.

  91

We carry the seeds of happiness with us wherever we go.

Martha Washington

Martha Washington was America's first First Lady. No wonder she gives us first-rate advice!

92

Happiness begins on the inside.

Marcus Aurelius

Marcus Aurelius was a Roman emperor who understood that happiness begins on the inside and works its way out.

Each day, look for a seed of excitement.

Barbara Jordan

Barbara Jordan served in the United States Congress.

Our happiness
depends upon
how we see
the world.

Leo Tolstoy

Leo Tolstoy was a
Russian writer.

If you keep telling yourself things are going to be bad, you'll probably be right.

Isaac Bashevis Singer

This quotation reminds us that it's better to expect the best than to fear for the worst.

96

If you think you can do it, you can do it.

Virgil

Believe in yourself with
all your heart!

Clear your mind of "can't."

Samuel Johnson

Believing in yourself is a very
wise thing to do.

Chapter 11
Dreaming Big Dreams

The future is your friend, so why not dream big? These words of wisdom remind us that if we can dream it, we can do it.

Dream big!

Conrad Hilton

Mr. Hilton, didn't just dream
big dreams, he built lots of
big hotels, too.

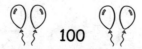

100

A Child's Book of Wisdom

You'll probably hit what you aim for, so why not aim high?

Henry David Thoreau

What you can dream,
you can do.

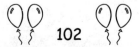

Whatever you are, be a good one.

Abraham Lincoln

Try to be the best you
you can be!

103

Great hopes make great people.

Thomas Fuller

Thomas Fuller was an English clergyman. A clergyman is a preacher, and Fuller was a wise one.

In hard times, we're saved by hope.

Menander

Menander was a Greek writer.
2500 years after he wrote
these words, they're still true.

Hope great hopes.

Robert Frost

Mr. Frost was a poet who inspired his generation with ideas like this.

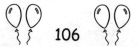

Dream glorious dreams, and as you dream, so shall you become.

John Ruskin

It's a strange secret:
You tend to become the person
you think you will become.

 107

Nothing happens unless it is first a dream.

Carl Sandberg

Before you do something, it helps to have a dream that you believe in.

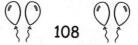

108

Chapter 12
Words to the Wise

In this final chapter, you'll be given some important advice from some very wise men and women. Happy reading!

When we do our best, miracles happen.

Helen Keller

Miss Keller's story is miraculous. If you don't know about her, go to the library and find out.

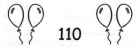

The best way to cheer yourself up is to cheer somebody else up.

Mark Twain

Mr. Twain reminds us that we make ourselves happy when we're kind to others.

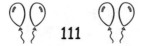

You can observe a lot just by watching.

Yogi Berra

Mr. Berra was a famous baseball player who knew a good thing when he saw it. You can, too, if you keep your eyes open.

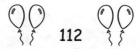

Wisdom is knowing what to overlook.

William James

William James, a famous American professor, was wise enough to know that some things aren't worth worrying about.

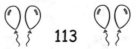

Do not worry about tomorrow....

A Child's Book of Wisdom

...Tomorrow can take care of itself.

The Bible
Matthew 6:34

This verse reminds us to take each day as it comes, because fretting about the future is useless.

Without faith, nothing is possible...

.......but.......

...with faith...

· · · · · · · · · · · · · · · · · ·

• • • • • • • • • • • • • • • • •

.......nothing is impossible!

Mary McLeod Bethune

Mary McLeod Bethune was a great teacher. These words were perhaps her greatest lesson.

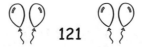

There is no limit on what God can make you.....if you are willing.

Oswald Chambers

So have faith in your future;
it's as bright as you decide
to make it.

The
End

About the Author

Criswell Freeman is a Doctor of Clinical Psychology who lives and works in Nashville, Tennessee. He is the author of numerous books including a series of quotation books by Delaney Street Press.

About Delaney Street Press

Delaney Street Press
is a publisher of
inspirational books.
If you'd like to know
more about us and
the books we publish,
please call
1-800-256-8584.